Dear
Little Ones

Book 3

Talking to Your Inner Children About Wholeness

Dear
Little Ones

Book 3

Jade Miller

illustrated by Germán Zaninetti

Published by
MultiFaceted
 Press

Cover and interior design by Christy Collins,
Constellation Book Design
Illustrated by Germán Zaninetti

ISBN (paperback): 978-1-7369902-4-7
ISBN (ebook): 978-1-7369902-5-4

Printed in the United States of America

Introduction

When I wrote the first *Dear Little Ones* book in 2015, I'd been blogging at *Thoughts From J8* for about a year. I wrote about dissociation, life as a multiple, and recovering from C-PTSD, trauma, ritual abuse, and attachment disorders. Someone in an online forum commented that they wished there were a book written for younger child self-states, and the idea intrigued me. Not too long after that, I wrote *Dear Little Ones Book 1: Hope, Help and Healing for Your Inner Children*.

The response to the book was unexpected. I hoped I would be able to sell enough copies to cover the publishing costs. But there were much bigger things in store for this book.

Within a year, *Dear Little Ones Book 1* had reached an international readership. It appeared on must-read lists of many grassroots trauma survivor networks all over the globe, from the U.S. to the United Kingdom to Australia. Trauma survivors, therapists, family members and friends of survivors were leaving positive reviews and sending emails to tell me how the book had touched them. And it didn't stop there.

Dear Little Ones Book 1 has been an Amazon bestseller numerous times since its original publication, and sales have consistently increased over time, despite my lack of marketing skills. This book has a special kind of magic.

My favorite emails are the ones I get from child self-states, shyly telling me that their therapist or another adult had read the book to them, and thanking me for helping them understand the world better.

I never intended for *Dear Little Ones* to become a series, but I often received emails from readers asking if I could write more books for inner children. So I wrote the second and third books in the series in 2016 and 2018, respectively.

I am thrilled that these books have made a positive difference to so many people's lives. I am even more thrilled that I have been able to create a healing resource for other survivors out of my lived experience of abuse and trauma. My hope for these books is that they reach far and wide and contribute to a generation of people that heals from their trauma and breaks the cycle of pain for generations to come.

L.R. Knost said, "Healing old hurts can only begin when the children we once were feel safe enough to speak their hearts to the adults we are now."

I hope that the *Dear Little Ones* books can help start these conversations.

Dear little ones,

I have one more thing to talk to you about.

Grab your blanket or your softie
if you want to, and snuggle up
one more time.

Are you ready?

I want to talk to you about being whole.

Being whole can mean more than one thing, but I want to talk to you about this:

One meaning of being whole is that nothing is missing.

For inside people, this can look like a lot of different things.

The important thing is to decide together what feels best to everyone inside you.

As you get to know everyone else inside, it's very important that they all get to choose.

Everyone gets a vote.

I like to think of my inside people
as my family.

Some people like to think of theirs
as a team, or a committee.

Some more words that other groups of inside people like to use are:

Council

Unit

Group

Squad

Tribe

Troop

Whatever name you like to use for your inside people is up to you.

It's important for everyone to know that each inside person is just as valuable as everyone else.

And they all need to be allowed to choose what being whole means for them.

Some inside families decide they all want to be joined together forever, and become one.

Some decide they want each member to remain separate.

Some groups decide that some members want to be joined, but some want to stay separate.

Whatever is right for everyone
inside you is the right choice
for your inside family.

No one has to do anything
they don't want to do.

No one else can decide what is best except you and your people.

Anyone who tries to tell you what choice is right for you needs to know that your people are the only ones who get to make that choice.

No one has to do anything
they aren't ready to do.

Many inside families have fears
about being whole, because they
think it means they will lose
someone.

They think it means some of the
members will have to die,
or go away.

But this is not true.

Being whole actually means
the opposite.

It means every member is there,
and every member counts.

Being whole means that as a group,
you are even more "you" than you
have ever been before!

And when you are all ready,
you all get to choose how to
live life all together.

You always get to choose.

Every member gets to choose.

Some members of your inside
family may be very tired.
They may have been doing
a difficult job for a long time.

They may want to rest.

And that is okay.

Some members may be ready to do new jobs, or keep doing their old job in a new way.

Those members may want their role in your inside group to stay the same.

And that is okay, too.

It may take some time to help
everyone decide what feels
best to them.

The important thing to know
is that no one needs to go away.

Being whole means everyone
matters, and everyone
gets to choose.

As you and your inside family decide what you each want to do, keep making choices that honor every inside part of you.

It may feel very different for a while.

It may take some time to get used to it.

But soon you will adjust to a new way of life that brings you even more healing and joy than you ever thought possible.

Being whole is possible.

Being whole can look however you and your inside family want it to.

Take as long as you need to decide what everyone inside needs.

You can do this.

I know that you are strong enough and smart enough to make the choices you need to make in order to live well.

I hope you never forget that you are *all* my heroes.

Love, Jade

And you can still write to me!

About the Author

JADE MILLER was born in east Tennessee. She is a survivor of ritual abuse and human trafficking, peer support worker, trauma recovery support group facilitator and author.

Jade has been writing since she was a young child, illustrating her own stories and winning writing awards in elementary school all the way through high school. She studied writing and editing in college, and made her publishing debut with the first *Dear Little Ones* book in 2015. Two additional *Dear Little Ones* books followed, as well as an ebook on attachment theory. Her books have been translated into several languages and have received international attention and praise from trauma survivors and therapists. She is also working on her first novel and a memoir.

Jade believes that the idea of one single cohesive "personality" is mostly a social construct. She suspects that universal multiplicity is much more likely—the concept that every person is a collection of self-states, and their upbringing and life experiences determine the level of awareness and cooperation between those self-states.

Jade is a peer support worker to people who identify as multiple or plural and/or have Dissociative Identity Disorder. She also offers education for mental health professionals drawing from her lived experiences and a private social media group for other multiples. Learn more about working with her one on one at www. peersupportformultiples.com. Jade's blog can be found at www.thoughtsfromj8.com.

For more information on the *Dear Little Ones* books, visit www.multifacetedpress.com.

About the Illustrator

GERMÁN ZANINETTI is an illustrator living in Argentina, where he studied for an illustrating career at Escuela de Artes Visuales Martin Malharro. He prefers to work on mythological themes (mostly Greek and Egyptian), but also feels comfortable with child themes. This is his first freelance project. You can email him at: harryzon88@gmail.com.

Made in United States
North Haven, CT
27 February 2023